HURRICANE WATCH

by Franklyn M. Branley
illustrated by Giulio Maestro

THOMAS Y. CROWELL   NEW YORK

LET'S READ-AND-FIND-OUT BOOK CLUB EDITION

The *Let's-Read-and-Find-Out Science Book* series was originated by Dr. Franklyn M. Branley, Astronomer Emeritus and former Chairman of The American Museum-Hayden Planetarium, and was formerly co-edited by him and Dr. Roma Gans, Professor Emeritus of Childhood Education, Teachers College, Columbia University.

Let's-Read-and-Find-Out Science Book is a registered trademark of Harper & Row, Publishers, Inc.

Library of Congress Cataloging in Publication Data
Branley, Franklyn Mansfield, 1915—
    Hurricane watch.

    (Let's-read-and-find-out science book)
    Summary: Describes the origin and nature of
hurricanes and ways of staying safe when threatened
by one of these dangerous storms.

    1. Hurricanes—Juvenile literature. [1. Hurricanes]
I. Maestro, Giulio, ill. II. Title. III. Series.
QC944.B7 1985   551.5'52   85—47534
ISBN 0-690-04470-4
ISBN 0-690-04471-2 (lib. bdg.)

The air that surrounds Earth weighs five quadrillion tons—that's 5,000,000,000,000,000 tons—believe it or not.

All the air around Earth = equals 5,000,000,000,000,000 tons

or: 1 quadrillion 5-ton elephants

It is always moving. When the air moves slowly,
there is only a light breeze. When it moves fast,
the wind blows hard.

If it blows faster than 74 miles an hour,
and covers about 500 miles, there is a hurricane.

Hurricanes are big, powerful and dangerous storms
that happen in August, September and October.
Most of them start in the Atlantic Ocean,
the Caribbean Sea and the Gulf of Mexico.

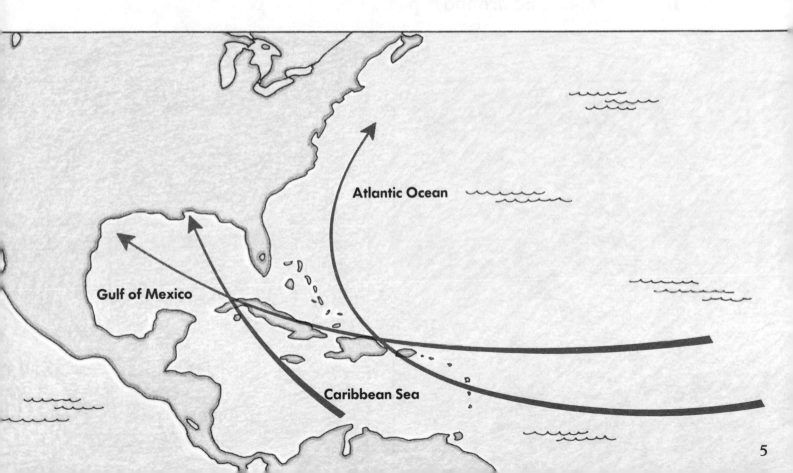

Atlantic Ocean

Gulf of Mexico

Caribbean Sea

These places get very warm, and so does the air above them. The warm air picks up a lot of water, and it rises.

Cooler air rushes in to take its place. The wind begins to blow. This air also gets warm, picks up water and rises. It goes around and around, up and up.

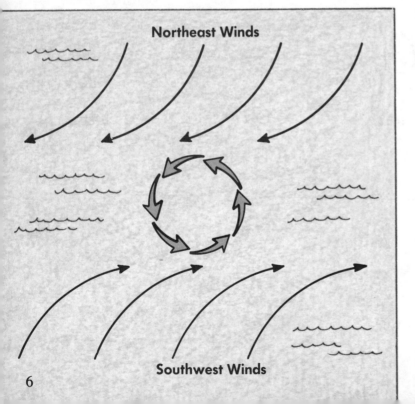

Northeast Winds

Southwest Winds

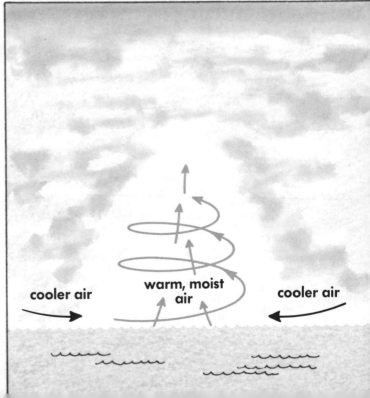

cooler air

warm, moist air

cooler air

At first, the wind blows slowly. More and more air rushes in. The wind blows harder and harder, faster and faster. Now it is a tropical storm.

Wind speed reaches 74 miles an hour. The tropical storm has become a hurricane. Wind speed goes higher and higher. It may blow one or two hundred miles an hour.

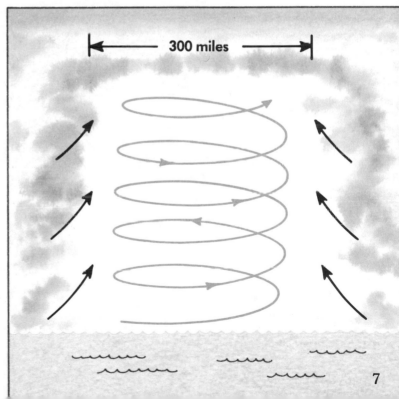

300 miles

Some hurricanes move over the ocean and never reach a seacoast. But some hurricanes move from the ocean toward the seacoast. The map shows paths that some hurricanes have followed.

1 Gladys, 1975
Center did not reach land.
Winds: 150–175 m.p.h.

2 Frederic, 1979
Worst hit areas: Southern Alabama, Southern Mississippi, Florida Panhandle. Winds: Up to 145 m.p.h.

3 Allen, 1980
Worst hit area: Southern Texas.
Winds: Up to 120 m.p.h.

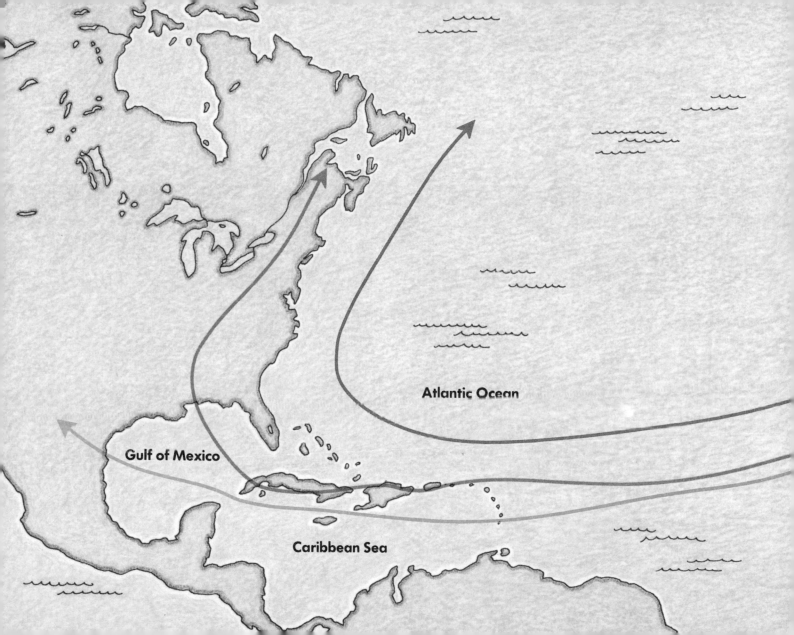

Atlantic Ocean

Gulf of Mexico

Caribbean Sea

The sky gets dark.
There may be thunder and lightning.
Then comes the rain.

It falls harder and faster. The wind blows
the rain sideways. Sewers fill up.
Water goes into cellars. Rivers and brooks overflow.
Streets and roads are flooded. Still the rain falls.

The wind pushes sea water toward the shore.
The water piles up, deeper and deeper. It may get 24 feet
higher than normal. It washes away sand and rocks.
The wind screams and howls.

It bends trees. Some are pulled out by the roots and knocked over. Roofs are torn from houses, and walls cave in. Whole houses are moved or turned around. And still the rain falls.

Cars are picked up and flipped over. Boats are carried into the streets. Electric wires are torn down.

Mobile homes are turned over and smashed.
Trees are blown down, or carried away by the heavy seas.

MOBILE HOMES FOR SALE

There is no way to stop a hurricane, so scientists
are trying to keep hurricanes from starting. They tried
spreading dry ice in the clouds. That may start rain falling
before a storm reaches the coast. It does not work very well,
so the only sure way to be safe is to get away from a hurricane.

Lucky for us, we have time to move away from the coast.
Hurricanes are not surprises. Weather satellites take
pictures of Earth and the clouds above it.

Heavy, dark clouds and strong winds may be the start of a hurricane. When weather watchers see the dark clouds take the shape of a doughnut, four or five hundred miles across, they start a hurricane watch.

Hour after hour, they keep track of the doughnut to see
if it is getting bigger, and which way the center
of the doughnut cloud is moving.

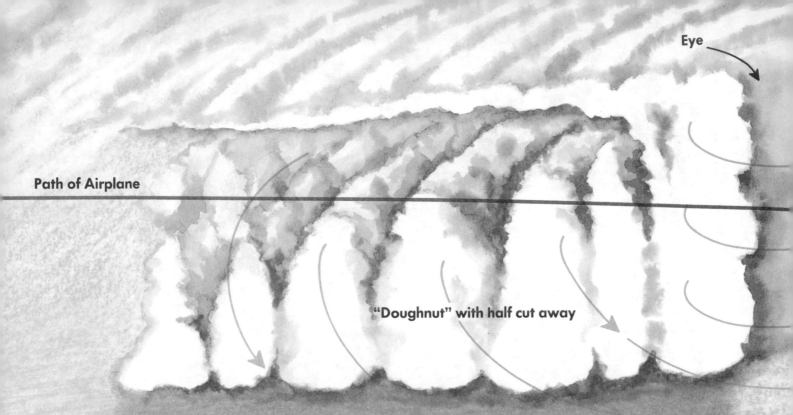

Eye

Path of Airplane

"Doughnut" with half cut away

Sometimes a weather plane flies right into the doughnut. The flight is rough and dangerous, but it is the only way to see how fast the wind is blowing. The plane flies into the "hole" of the doughnut, which is called the eye of the hurricane. There the air is calm. Sunlight may stream into it.

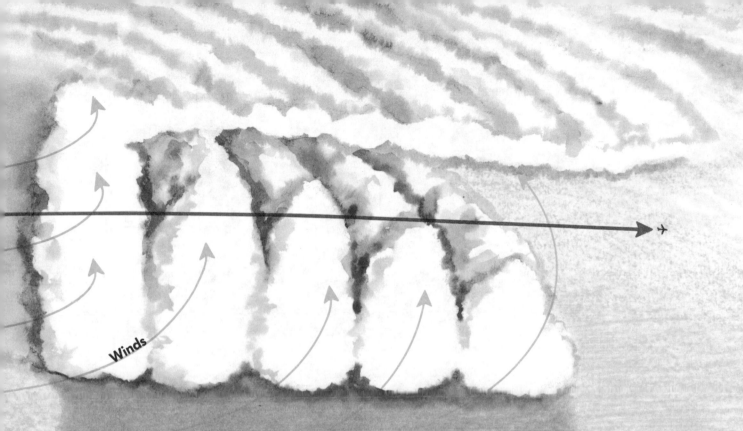

Winds

But the plane keeps going, right through the clouds
and out the other side. Instruments in the plane measure
air temperature, pressure, and how much water
there is in the clouds.

Weather watchers then get on the radio and television
and tell people about the storm. It is moving toward
the shore, they say, so get ready for it.

People cover windows with boards. They take chairs
and tables indoors.

They sail boats into safe harbor, and tie them with extra strong ropes. They put heavy cables over mobile homes.

Most important of all: people move out.
They get into their cars and drive away from the coast.
They go inland. They move out before the storm hits.

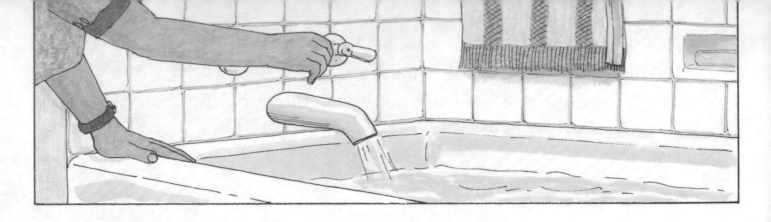

If you cannot leave your house, there are things you must do. Water and gas pipes may get broken, so run water into your bathtub. Electricity will probably go off. Make sure you have a flashlight, a battery radio, candles and dry matches.

Tape windows so they won't shatter. Then keep away from the windows. And stay indoors.

The storm may last for several hours. Then, all at once, the wind dies down. You are in the eye of the hurricane. After the eye passes, the wind blows again. More rain falls, just as hard as before.

When the hurricane is over, wind speed drops. The rain stops. All is quiet. The radio tells you the storm is over.

You can return to your house and start cleaning up. If electric wires are on the ground, don't touch them.

Every year there are hurricanes. Some are worse than others. People lose their houses. Some lose their lives.

Those who listen for warnings and follow directions are safe. They move away from the shore, where most damage occurs.

We cannot stop a hurricane. But we can get out of its way. We can move to a safe place, and stay there until the storm is over.